Excerpt from Casual Day at the Crazy House

...Within a week, Dad had moved into the bathroom. There, thanks to wireless and his cell, he continued running his company. Nobody seemed to think all this was as weird as I did. "The energy in the house is imbalanced," Mom had said, pushing out a laugh. Gammy got an inward look. "There always was more to him. Give it time."

Now he grinned at me like the old Dad. "So you and Zach are officially a non-item. Any other young men on your horizon?"

"No." My heart flipped like a fish.

"I'm sure they notice you."

"Dad. Are you coming to my graduation?"

"Oh, honey..." He stared into the Cheezit bowl. I pounded the doorframe with my fist, felt it crack a little, and slammed down the stairs.

For my father,
James Davis Wilson

The Beautiful Name: Four Stories

by

Helen W. Mallon

Copyright © 2014 Helen W. Mallon
Books to Go Now Publication

Cover Design by Jane Reed Wilson

All rights reserved

ISBN-978-1500821999
ISBN-10: 1500821993

CONTENTS

Did You Put the Cat to Bed?
7

"You Say You Want a Revolution"
34

Casual Day at the Crazy House
54

Pertaining to My Arrest for Indecent Exposure
84

Did You Put the Cat to Bed?

Izzy put the twins to bed in the cribs that were supposed to have been exchanged for beds six months ago when they turned three. Because for ages, Harris had been saying *we'll shop once I get a handle on this deadline*, but he never did get a handle. And they didn't shop. His deadlines left him staring in bafflement at the latest underestimated job-hour projection scope on his computer screen.

Izzy ran water in the bathtub. She was not, dammit, going to let him slither out of his promise to help her buy the beds. She tested the water with her toe. Reese opened the bathroom door to complain that he couldn't straighten out his legs in his cage, which is what the twins had taken to calling their cribs.

"Heave out the teddy bears if you want more room," Izzy said, shivering. She eased into the tub. She expected one or both of her sons to return, but she must have already put them to bed enough times tonight, because neither one did. She closed her eyes to the flumping sound of plush toys hitting window glass. Her lower back was kinked tight, and she tried using a rubber duck as a massage tool, but it was too *beaky*.

Relax, she told herself, *you've been waiting all day for this*, but it wasn't happening. She scrubbed a splotch of yellow wall paint off her hand.

When she felt waterlogged, she pulled herself out of the tub, dried off with a possibly clean towel, and used it to wipe the full-length mirror.

From the neck down, she was surprisingly fine. Aside from the intriguing earth-colored line where sweat now ran from her navel to her pubic area, pregnancy with twins had added nothing except a pleasing fullness to her breasts. She'd lost her life-long baby fat. The little pad under her chin had resolved into a clean line. Apparently, she was still pretty.

Were her eyes really askew? She closed one. If something didn't change, she'd begin to resemble a Picasso portrait of a dis-arranged woman, with both eyes where her left ear used to be. She conjured from memory. She hadn't had the chance to look at an actual Picasso in a thousand years. The back view, she had to say, wasn't bad. Her butt was firmer than it used to be.

What was wrong with her?

And why had Harris gone skittish on sex? She'd had her tubes tied right after the twins were born. Their sporadic lovemaking dripped with unnecessary spermicide, but he insisted on it. You'd think he'd been the only one walloped by the pregnancy. In fact the sight of twin embryos, like grapes with urgently swimming arms and legs on the video monitor, had made Izzy feel something like frostbite.

But they learned to deal. At least they tried.

Now Izzy sat in the hall wrapped in her stained terrycloth robe and listened to the boys sleep. Harris was a good provider. He always paid the bills on time, even though he seriously undercharged his clients. He would never, as Izzy's last live-in boyfriend had done, sell off her stereo equipment to obtain money for reefer. Harris didn't actually know what pot smelled like. His apartment had been right above Izzy's, in a ten-story brick building by a train station. A few days after Bobby, well, vanished, with her Sony MHC and two hundred dollars in cash in the middle of the night, Harris lugged her sagging, reefer-burned sofa down to the lobby and off to the nearest city dump in a U-Haul. He insisted on paying for the dump, because he was Harris.

She remembered his baffled eyes before he turned the ignition key. "I was under the impression you guys were burning incense down there," he'd said. Izzy's heart expanded with warmth at this childlike man who stared at your chin when he talked to you.

Now one of the twins rolled over in his cage, thwacking the bars. Izzy pressed her hands to her face. Her 10 p.m. headache trickled up the back of her neck.

It wasn't Bobby who had knocked her up, nor any of Bobby's three predecessors. These had been spontaneous-combustion types with the starved physiques of 1970s British rockers. Their very names roused flames of indignation in the eyes of Izzy's father, Maurice Williams. No, Harris was the man Dad favored.

Harris was kind and steady. When Izzy told her father about the dusky kiss at the end of the U-haul day, knowing he would approve of her new friend, she didn't say why she had kissed Harris. That talking about drugs had evidently pained him and she was grateful for his help in ridding the apartment of Bobby's flotsam. She saw loneliness in Harris's over washed, poly/cotton shirt and blue utility pants. The language of caress was one Izzy had figured he'd understand. *Understanding* was an understatement. He'd actually *asked*, 'Is this all right? Do you mind?' And with all that, after some anxious feints he knew right where to put his lost-boy lips, and he kissed smooth like caramel.

Harris was such a switch for Izzy that her fellow art students enthused as if dating him was an act of radical performance art. Sometimes after a 16-hour day at his computer, Harris would show up at her door with containers of Chinese takeout. He took photographs at her Senior painting show reception and charmed her parents.

In the end, her pregnancy felt scripted, especially since they'd been using protection. Especially when Izzy's mother called to break the news of her father's liver cancer. Izzy went home that morning and stayed until he died.

"He's a good man," Maurice Williams had said, shaken like an old tree that would not break beneath its years. "He should do the honorable thing."

"I can't," Izzy wept. "I can't think marriage. Not with you sick."

Her father, who had just had lab work done, pulled the pale Band-Aid from his arm. "How employable are you?"

"I couldn't live with Harris. All he *does* is work!"

Her father's eyes were the color of earth. Izzy almost saw the shadows of God-fearing ancestors waiting mute for her decision. He repeated her words. "*All* he does?"

"I always thought I had time before..." Time to play. A few more years of la la la. Since her parents had always worked so hard, and she knew this was her path, too. But not yet. "Please," she said. He was still the largest person she knew. "I should be comforting you."

"Baby girl," but he shook his head and pushed her away. "Didn't I always say you can do anything you set your mind to?"

Within a year of his diagnosis, Izzy did three impossible things. She kissed her father in his coffin. She married a kind man she didn't love. Four months later, she gave birth to twins, with minimal use of drugs.

This past week, the boys' pediatrician had told Izzy that the nighttime headaches sounded like stress. Izzys' mother suggested a couple shots of whiskey before the twins went down for the night. Izzy fired back, *For me or them?* Her own doctor said no, not with the meds he was about to prescribe, and *let's give it a month, shall we?*

Izzy returned to the bathroom. She took her conservatively prescribed dosage, which left twenty-two pills. How many pills would she need to take to convince Harris: Life wasn't working?

"*Asshole.* You call yourself a computer?" Up in his office, Harris yelled at his Hewlett- Packard, which he had named Bill Gates. He was trying to make up for lost time. He'd taken the boys to the playground that afternoon while Izzy approximated a nap. He worked around the clock, trying to reconcile his inner genius with the fact that he was paid by soulless corporations. He was always, almost, on to something.

Izzy pulled her sash tight and took the stairs to the third floor. Harris squinted at Bill Gates and lifted his chin slightly, which meant he knew she stood in the doorway. He looked his most white in front of the screen. His face glimmered, as he generated code on his computer to steal information from people who used computers to steal information from soulless corporations. His fine brown hair, cowlicked over his eyebrow, was especially white. Perhaps the Scottish ancestral memory in his blood rose to the surface when he sat at the computer, absorbed in what he insisted were the tribal intricacies of logic, making him pale.

Izzy felt the *blackness* inside her. The small nut of African genetics that was rooted, she believed, in the earth of her mind farthest from her husband's, giving her skin its beautiful mocha tint, and which she had passed on to the boys, undiluted. She was proud to drive them to the Pathmark, where few white people shopped, even though Harris complained that they came home smelling like something fried.

Harris didn't look up. Exhaustion traveled up from Izzy's heels, and her head throbbed like she'd run into a cinderblock wall.

She had screamed at the twins, Willis and Reese, tonight when she found a hunk of dried- up cheese hidden under a sofa cushion. She hadn't bothered with the supper dishes, she shook one of the boys—which one was it? God, they were both predatory in turn— when they wouldn't stop chasing the cat. She'd kicked open the kitchen door, and exploded a plate as hard as she could against the concrete slab where the trashcans overflowed in bacterial glory while the boys, again, watched *Pranks on the Pros*.

Izzy had put the twins to bed with bottles of watered-down juice to keep them quiet, and after they gave up thumping their feet on the crib rails in their nighttime ritual of preschool machismo, thumping until it must have hurt, she lay in the tub and imagined sugar-pits in their perfectly formed teeth.

Now, looking at her husband, she whispered his name.

"What?" He jerked toward her, but his eyes didn't gel, as if she were a TV set on mute and her voice came from another source.

"Harris," Izzy said firmly. "I used to be an artist. My brain has desiccated to the size and texture of a gummy bear. I am stressed. I'm seriously thinking of taking an overdose. I am thinking of having myself committed."

"Come again?" Harris blinked. "What time is it?" He looked from her to the wall clock, and back again. Then he asked, "Did you put the cat to bed?"

Izzy stared. He wouldn't cope. Harris *could not* cope. She tugged her bathrobe close. "Bag it," she said, and went down to the sofa in the TV room to pretend to sleep.

The next morning, Harris left for Starbucks to meet the geek who was the other half of his current project. Izzy was making peanut butter and jelly sandwiches for the boys' three-times-weekly socialization at a preschool in the local AME Church, when Willis tugged on her University of the Arts sweatshirt.

As she bent down, he snaked a fat arm around her neck. Willis crooned in her ear and gave her four messy kisses. He trembled with life. Reese hurtled over, almost knocking her down. The twins bloomed in her arms. They were sturdy cherubs. They were love incarnate. They broke away to chase the tabby, who was so fed up she growled and scratched Reese on the back of his hand. Both boys set to wailing. After the comforting and the tossing outside of the cat, the washing of hands and several Band-Aids per child, Izzy called the veterinarian to say, *Rip her claws out*. But all she got was a voice recording saying that due to unforeseen circumstances, emergency calls were being taken by some vet out in the suburbs.

Izzy looked at the boys, who were playing with a stinkbug they'd found on the floor. This was it. She felt carbonated. She picked up the phone to call her mother, with whom, as of this moment, she no longer had 'issues.' It was Friday. The twins would eat Happy Meals and throw French fries at Nascar or *Animal*

House on one of her mother's zillion cable channels and sleep in their clothes and not brush their teeth and have Froot Loops for lunch and probably taste Coors Lite, but at least they'd be alive on Sunday evening.

Maurice Williams, grave, courtly and the color of Ghirardelli milk chocolate, had known when to keep his mouth shut and had been a restraining influence on her mother. You could have balanced a carpenter's level between his eyes.

After dropping the boys at Tots 'n Tykes, Izzy inspected the seat belts in her mother's low-slung Eldorado, then installed their car seats. "We're going to a B and B out in New Hope," she lied, and went back into her mother's house to make sure her cell phone number was written smack on the wall by the phone.

"Whuz' up, yo?" her mother asked, with a nicotine grin. "You gettin' your groove back." Izzy loathed it when her mother talked street, but she tried to interpret it as loyalty to the memory of her father. Never mind that Maurice Williams would sooner have missed church than indulge in such an idiom. Izzy took the opportunity to test out her most radiant smile, as if her mother was a man she'd just met. Mom patted her on the bottom. "I promise not to smoke in the house," she said.

When Izzy returned home, Harris stood at the sink washing dishes. With the sponge dripping on the floor, he said that due to circumstances beyond his control, i.e., the Starbucks geek had crapped out on him, he had to go to New York that afternoon. He'd walk the six blocks to the train station with his overnight bag.

"That's okay," she said. "The boys are going to my mother's for the weekend, and I'm gonna enjoy myself. Maybe go out with some friends."

"Well." He looked at the peanut-buttery knife. "You work harder than I do."

Izzy drove him to 30th Street Station for a direct connection to the New York train. He kissed her lingeringly in short-term parking, where there was no possibility of escalation into pregnancy-risk behavior. His lips lacked muscle tone. He said he'd be home before Saturday night. Izzy promised to replenish his supply of Pepto Bismol. He was so grateful that as he walked away, she wanted to slam him to the ground. Why didn't he turn and ask who she'd be with? She watched him struggle with the heavy brass door before he disappeared into the vast station.

Her next stop was Sans Limites in gentrified Manayunk, where the clothing was vintage. She tried on and bought a completely sassy dress and what her mother would describe as "fuck-me shoes." The dress was red and Seventies and low-cut and the black shoes were all sharp points.

"Are you from Italy?" asked the saleslady, and Izzy laughed. At Bucks County Coffee, she drank a frappo-something and fielded a call from her mother.

No, Izzy told her, it would not be cute if the twins each got an ear pierced at the mall after daycare. At least she asked.

She went home and took off her wedding ring and slept. A comatose sleep, aided only by the prospect of sin. When she got up, she made the bed and took a long shower. Izzy stood in her ratty bathrobe and blew her hair out long and shiny for the first time in forever. She ate a Power Bar and put on the red dress and invisible stockings and the fuck-me shoes and brushed her teeth. Onyx earrings, no necklace. She had a great collarbone.

Izzy mostly remembered to breathe as she drove downtown to Condom Nation on South Street, where she procured a box of your basic tasteful rubbers. Her lizard-skin purse now full of surgical latex, she nudged through hideous traffic going south and parked under a bridge.

She almost missed Warmdaddy's, tucked away behind a multiplex theater, but its reflective, darkened-glass exterior promised zydeco and anonymity, and a vending machine of men. Hadn't her father said she could accomplish anything she put her mind to? It was a long time since she'd had a groove. All right, a dangerous groove. Even her chain-smoking mother would question her judgment at this moment, reciting the case *just Tuesday* of the Center City woman who had been raped *in her own hallway*. Izzy was so alert that she felt the sidewalk's texture through her fuck-me shoes. There would be a man. She knew it. She stopped. A buzzing noise commenced in her head.

She called her mother and left a message for the twins, saying she could eat them up and that she would check for messages often. Their taste for McDonalds' forbidden fries was appealing enough, they wouldn't pine for her.

Dangerous. Go.

Indoors, Warmdaddy's glimmered twilight. The fortyish man in the slim suit at the bar was with a white man who punched him on the chest and laughed and got up to leave. The white guy had a *je ne sais quois* that suggested gayness. He walked past Izzy without looking up from his Blackberry.

Izzy had a hunch the man with his elbows on the shining bar was her man because he was dressed precisely enough to be gay, too, even though this was Warmdaddy's, Mecca of jazz and machismo. Since she was turning things inside out, it stood to reason that the man who picked her up would be more than appearance suggested. But that was crazy. *Her* appearance was wrong, she felt, too flashy for a man in a slim taupe suit. She perched on a stool at the farthest end of the bar from him.

Without looking away from the bartender simultaneously pouring two whiskies, Izzy sensed the man closing in behind her.

"May I buy you a drink?" He sounded like a movie actor she couldn't quite identify. The man was fit and expensive and a television producer in town for something to do with John Coltrane. He knew how to wear gold against his sable wrist. She drank a Cosmopolitan and they looked at a close-up of a woman Izzy ought to know singing in bruised-looking eye shadow on one of the TV sets above the bar. The man's hair was cleanly cropped, his fingers long. He knew the bartender and the bartender pretended that he'd seen Izzy before, tossing out *it's been a while*.

"I'm a graduate student in painting," she told the sable man, which might actually be true someday.

"I'm going to go out on a limb," the man replied, which likely meant he was married, from the way his hands opened to catch the word 'limb.' He had a velvet voice that resembled neither her father's Moses-down-from-the-mountain bass or Harris's fussy diction. She thought the man was going to invite her to have firecracker shrimp in the dining room and hang around for zydeco, but she found herself, ten minutes later, strapped into the slippery leather seat of his black Mercedes, listening to squiggly Coltrane and looking at a fleck of yellow paint that remained on her pinky nail after repainting the kitchen wall last week following the debacle involving the twins and frozen blueberries.

Yikes. I'm doing it. Perhaps he would spirit her across the river and deep into the Jersey Pine Barrens to hack her to shreds. She checked her phone. Which was the emergency button? She planted her thumb on it and swallowed hard. *Cut the doubts.* Desperate times called for outrage.

The man slung his casual wrist on the steering wheel and looked her over with a smile that suggested the whole thing had been her idea. He opened his jacket, revealing a crisp shirtfront. "No weapons," he said. "No harm intended."

Izzy sat back, and a hot, expansive feeling spread while her heart knocked and the Mercedes oozed to a stop at a red light. A guy crossed the street in front of them and looked first at her, then stared at the man with rank and file envy.

Are you from Italy? Izzy laughed, remembering the sales girl's question. The sable man slid her an approving look.

The ride was barely fifteen minutes. The car glided onto a cobblestone drive under a hotel awning, and a valet whisked it away. The lobby was plush and soundless. The man's room on the eleventh floor was so neat, she thought he must have prearranged with the concierge to come back to a different, unused, room every night. But when he took off his jacket and brushed it, she saw his suits hanging in the closet like waiting staff members. There were eight of them, arranged from light to dark. It made her faint with longing to think that some people lived in such a state of order. The man touched a sleek box and borderline-familiar jazz slid around as he poured two glasses of

Black Bush over ice that seemed to materialize from the wall.

You're not going to fall in love with him, Izzy told herself. *It's just the suits.* It was the way he tied his shoes after he took them off, then slid them under the bed. It was the non-Harris musculature of his chest. He turned off the lights and found the side zipper of her dress, quickly, as if by sonar.

The foreplay wasn't entirely sexual; while he took almost as much pleasure in handling her clothes as he did in her breasts, it felt like gym class, or the way she thought porn actors must feel sometimes. A matter of arranging yourself. Not that the suave man didn't know what he was doing; but Izzy was aware of her elbows and knees. He produced a condom from a little grey case in the nightstand, and she was glad she hadn't fumbled for one in her lizard-skin bag.

I'm breaking it, she told herself. *That Commandment.*

He traveled the length of her with his firm lips and the sheets moved creamy against her feet. She tried to pretend she was Alice Coltrane on the road with John, but she wished the sable man wouldn't be so gentle. He played her like the keys of a saxophone. He ought to leave a bruise or two for Harris to find, the overbloom of her tell-tale heart. She could inform her husband outright that she'd had a fling. But why should she have to be the one to notice things *for* him?

"Relax," the man said, and nuzzled her neck, then circled his fingers between her legs in a swimmy way and so she was liking it, but that wasn't really the point, and she sighed in the whiskey dark and trailed her fingers along his chest. "Would you hurt me just a little?" she asked, now that it was definite he wasn't going to kill her.

"Ah, baby," he said. "I'm sorry. That's not my thing."

He was pretty good. He provided her with memories. His hands glided as if she were a bolt of silk. He slid into her like a plastic sword into its sheath, and he came with a groan.

The man kissed her on the cheek and went into the bathroom. Ten minutes later, smiling gently, with a glistening streak of water on his bicep and wrapped in a towel, he handed her a fresh terrycloth robe, so thick it weighed as much as one of her kids. Since he had gone first, Izzy took her time in the bathroom, which was immaculate and well-provided with little bottles of stylish product. In the steaming tub, she checked her phone messages.

None.

The little boys would have fallen asleep by now to the rhythms of women firing their machine-gun bras in *Austin Powers*, one of her mother's favorites. It would take three weeks of unadulterated Mr. Rogers to get that out of their systems. Three weeks of Nothing Changes, which would become three years, then five, *ad* forever, amen. She laid her head, which was beginning to hurt, against the back of the tub. The bathroom was so white it reminded her of that tunnel of light people see after they die.

When she returned to the bedroom in the luxurious robe with wet hair finger-combed down her back, the man already slept, lying half-covered on his side. His eyelashes were thick and curly, like a child's. In the light from the bathroom, Izzy found her dress and panty hose and underwear, neatly arranged, and she dressed silently, sitting on a chair to work the shoes back on. She saw a pair of nail scissors beside a metallic toiletries kit. She clipped off a lock of her hair. She laid the hair on his pillow, then studied the clean lines of his face.

The night had cost the elegant man nothing.

Would nothing rouse Harris?

Her thumb probed the open blade. She pulled it across her forearm—*quick, Harris. I'll make you look*—but felt no sting and no moisture of blood. She returned to the bathroom and tried the other blade, sawing it back and forth. Either the scissors were dull or her resolve was weak. She opened the medicine cabinet and then pawed through his toiletries kit, but found nothing; of course, the man would go to a barber.

Sitting on the closed toilet, Izzy made an experimental stab at her thigh through the sheer pantyhose. She closed her eyes and tried again. Ten times. Hard enough that it hurt down to her foot, but while the hose ripped, she couldn't break the skin. There would be nothing for Harris to react to. Maybe a few red spots that she would have to interpret for him even if she snuck her naked thigh under his nose like an actress in some audition that wasn't going to end well.

Izzy examined the scissors. She looked at their slipcase and found a store receipt neatly folded beside it. How could she, of all people, have missed it? Was the metal in her hand so familiar that she assumed the ability of a pair of blunt-ended child's manicure scissors to sever a marriage? Past tired, she put the child-safe scissors away. In the bedroom, the man, perhaps a father himself or a solicitous uncle, had rolled over on his back. He half-smiled in his loose heaviness. Would he remember her?

"So," she said.

Izzy yanked open the door, which was lighter than she expected. Stepping into the hall, she slammed it as hard as she could and felt the reverberation up to her collarbone.

From the hotel room came nothing but silence.

A large man standing by the elevator looked up sharply. He was older, a man of authoritative demeanor with gazing eyes, lighter-skinned than the sable man. For a terrible moment, Izzy saw her father, Maurice Williams, arisen. Her headache flourished.

The big man wore a tailored suit with an unbuttoned collar, and he held the door open when the elevator arrived. His jowled sympathy made her feel like a teenage runaway. Izzy stepped into the box of the elevator. It wouldn't have bothered her if this stranger had resembled Harris. If he had *been* Harris, it would have been perfect.

A husband can be anyone, but you only have one father to push you in the wrong direction. Her dad had never met Willis and Reese, his namesakes, the only reason Harris mattered. Izzy stood in front of the tall man, and in her fist she gripped the finger that bore a spot of yellow paint. Her crotch was moist, and she wondered if anything showed through her dress. She held her breath, while her angry legs trembled.

The elevator stopped at the third floor, where there was an ice machine. "Goodnight, then." The stranger's voice was bland, perhaps carefully so, and he exited. The elevator fell with Izzy in its icy light, descending farther than it felt possible to go in the high-rise.

You can do anything you set your mind to, she repeated. But how do you argue your case with a man who is dead?

"You Say You Want a Revolution"

Cape Cod, 1972

Mark knew that Sarah would be a teenager about their meeting time, so he poked in shops along Water Street then walked over the rusty drawbridge in the fog. Rich, olive-colored water slapped the hulls of yachts and Beetle Cats in the harbor. Woods Hole's grey-shingled roofs were softened by grainy moisture, and log jammed cars lined the narrow streets. Mark returned to the parking lot of the motel where he'd arrived a few hours ago and stood just inside the open vestibule at the rear of the Tide n' Time, waiting.

Mark was a science and math teacher at the Quaker school where Sarah had finished tenth grade.

He was taking a significant risk by giving her what she wanted. She had begged him to come down to the Cape. She had called repeatedly from a pay phone at the village market:

God, I miss you. There's nothing to do here. Mark knew that ten years earlier, he would have seriously risked getting fired. But the whole world was loosening up, the winds of social experimentation had swept through the school, and Mark hoped that finding his way through the seams of convention would help him feel like a man. He liked to joke that married couples were splitting and recoupling like atoms, while hair sprouted in women's armpits and on the heads of Negro students. Mark was all for bra burning. Two years ago, the headmaster where Mark taught had shucked his first wife for a sweet-faced teacher in a miniskirt; all very discreetly done, but shucking was the bottom line.

Messing around was the furthest thing from Mark's mind when Sarah came to him for math tutoring. But her long brown hair as she sat beside him in the tiny study room had reflected tints of roan, even peach. Then without anyone moving, the fluorescent light overhead stopped buzzing. She looked up at him, startled, as if he had caused the silence. Not that he had spoken or inclined the slightest bit toward her as he watched Sarah work. He was hardly even breathing. So Mark convinced himself that by lifting her head, it was she who had seduced him. In her widened eyes, boundaries fell away.

The vestibule of the Tide 'n Time smelled quick and fresh, a distillation of the beach. Mark's heart expanded with the rightness of Sarah. She was so young she didn't know what normal male performance was. After all, she had never seemed disappointed when he lost it halfway through sex.

Mark happened to be facing the right way when Sarah glided out of the mist on the sidewalk, pushing her bicycle. Like a sea bird, he thought, riding on water, not bound to earth. Sarah wore cutoffs. She had bare feet even in the town, and he shook his head. What was she thinking?

She smiled her curvy smile and shook the hair out of her face, but they didn't touch. They were still outside.

Sarah felt so relieved. Mark was *there*. He'd come for her. His hair had grown over his collar, making him look younger than thirty-five. The last time she saw him, about a month ago, she had told him how cute he would look with longer hair. All I did was mention it, she thought. He *listened.* He heard me. Mark took a step, his hand raised toward her face, but he flushed, glancing around the parking lot with an embarrassed dip of his head.

"Come to the room," he said, and Sarah felt a tremor down her spine. He wheeled her bike to a pole and unwound the lock. She had worked her alibi around a James Bond movie with her brother Will and her brother's friend, whose parents were out of town. The teacher would drop her off at the friend's house around eleven tonight, and Sarah's father had said he would pick her and Will up in the station wagon "after the movie was over," but Sarah knew this really meant *when Dad and his girlfriend were done being alone together*. Sarah's brother was good to her. He had helped her lie to her dad. Will didn't like the teacher, but this was what brothers did.

At school, Sarah was quiet and she thought boys didn't notice her, but something hidden and fierce in her, convinced of their indifference, sought forbidden walls to scale. She was done with immature kids. She had vaulted over all of them with this new kind of love that made her feel she was part of the movements, the powers and liberations that were blowing like winds through everyone's hair. Still, in the past few weeks, she couldn't get an old song out of her head, and before Mark arrived, this afternoon she had walked on the fog-chilled, empty beach, singing *Brandy* to herself, a song about the "fine girl" many sailors would have married, but for the sea's restless claim. She envied Brandy because one man had given her a chain of "finest silver from the south of Spain." But now, she reassured herself, Mark had driven all this way just to see her.

The motel room was white and damp, musty-smelling, as if it had been cleaned with tatters of fog. "Did you bring me anything?" Sarah teased. But she was sorry, because he had been holding her—the kiss had made the ache open between her legs—and the question made him draw back. She wanted the hard reassurance of his shoulder against her cheek.

"All in good time," and he gathered up her hair and brought it to his nose. "You should have worn some shoes," he added, glancing at her dirty feet.

Will he buy me some? Sarah wondered, but she only said, "I like your hair long." "Huh," he responded, sliding a hand past his collar. "I'm overdue for a haircut." Sarah dropped onto the rough synthetic bedspread. He had forgotten that she liked his hair long. She lay back so he wouldn't notice her disappointment. She hovered in whiteness. Walls, furniture, everything in the room was a shade of white. The bed moved unnaturally, like a soft plank. Mark leaned over and kissed her, and Sarah gave him the best open-mouthed kiss she could. When his pinkie ring caught in her hair, he freed it, gently smiling. She touched the small lines around his eyes, but when he stared down inside her with his peculiar hunger that was close to panic, she felt her eyes click away. Her eyes were like polarized magnets, unable to remain on his. She sat up. She feared he would think she didn't love him.

Mark liked the way she looked out from behind long, untrimmed hair, as if seeking someone to hunt her. Hers was the adolescence he had never had, working every spare minute in his father's hardware store when he was a teenager and in college. Then his ex-wife had gotten pregnant on the second date, before they'd even had real sex, trapping him. Mark's son was in college, but he hadn't seen him in almost a year.

"Hey," he told Sarah. "I won't bite." Sarah took this reassurance to mean that he wanted to stay with her. She relaxed and inhaled his smell of good, faded cologne and travel sweat. Afterwards it would permeate her skin and she could wear him home, like an invisible garment, and she matched her breath to his.

Slowly, he kissed her neck. He knew how to prime her. But he knew he was the one with the problem, and anxiety set off a vein of headache in his skull.

Sarah felt swimmy and loose. "I asked and here you are!" She spoke as if she had whisked him here by overwhelming force of delight. Relief washed over Mark. He peeled off the girl's clothes with her help. She unbuttoned his shirt, and he raked his eyes over her body, trying not to think of the ensuing mechanics. This might be it, Mark thought. If anything, she had grown more womanly since he last saw her naked.

Warm in the coarse sheets, half-proud, half-ashamed and melted but numb, Sarah touched him, offered her breasts, adjusting her body.

But when he entered her with the rubber on, they pumped in a mechanical way. It was the same old thing. He was unable to keep going.

"Please," he said, "don't let me lose it." "I'm trying," she said, rocking with him. "I know. It isn't you."

She never laughed at him.

Sarah didn't really understand what it meant that men came—she had learned about it in health class, but that school topic bore no connection to the musty room and the teacher's weight pressing into her. She thought the teacher wanted to keep pumping indefinitely, not realizing he had a specific goal in mind. She wanted to please him, but she always relaxed when he quit.

Though he was heavy on her, she might have been floating in the musty evening glimmer as if in space. After a while, he gave up and rolled away with a groan. He fell asleep and his eyes glittered, half open, so she turned and lay on her side, studying her arm as if it belonged to someone else. Her skin was very pale; unlike the other girls in her class, she never tanned. Mark had assured her that the hippies had it right, that someday their philosophy would take over. Someday no one would care about superficial things like whether you tanned, or how old you should be before you could have sex.

He snored a little. She tried to doze. With their legs tangled up together, it looked like they'd traded parts of themselves. She touched his lower lip, which was full like a half moon. The room filled with twilight. She tried to imagine that his sleep could filter into her through the pores in their legs, like some kind of drug, but as the darkness increased she became more alert. At the same time, she felt too tired to get up and look out the window, so she was half-glad there was nothing to see in the fog.

When Mark woke up he switched on the lamp, which hurt her eyes. "I'll take you to a special place I know," he said, "after we eat. But you need shoes." He pulled on his pants, then he combed her hair with his fingers, murmuring *Pretty, Pretty,* as she sat on the edge of the bed, looking toward the window and the shapeless night. She smiled, thinking of the shoes.

They went to a shop on the Water Street, and he chose a pair of plastic flip-flops. Her throat tightened but she thanked him, not telling him she had hoped for a pair of huaraches with sewn-on beads that they'd seen in the window. He added a shell bracelet and paid for everything.

Out on the street, Mark thought she was thrilled with her gifts, as she examined the hollows of the shells in the bracelet. He felt cheap and shabby. He knew that getting a sixteen- year old to love you was not such a great accomplishment, and that someday Sarah would resent him. They walked in silence.

On a restaurant deck overlooking the harbor, two ladies poked at their dinner salads at the table next to Mark and Sarah. They were women about Mark's age, self-consciously groomed and polished, and one of them kept glancing at them. He ran his hands through his uncut hair. The women whispered together, but when he challenged them by returning a stare, they looked ostentatiously away. Mark and Sarah ate hamburgers and fries, and he made a point of laughing as Sarah threw breadcrumbs to the mallard ducks that paddled in and out of the fog.

The ducks made Sarah feel sad, so she laughed even harder as she threw the bread. The teacher noticing the women. To make them think that Sarah was his daughter, he started praising the girl for her last report card of the year. The women stood up to leave, their faces carefully neutral, smoothing their skirts. Mark sputtered into silence as they walked away. "Sarah?" She was leaning over the railing now in her cutoffs, watching something in the water. Mark couldn't help staring at her ass, like a peach in her cutoff shorts. "You're not listening," he accused. Her indifference to his praise had caused a glassy feeling to rise in his chest.

She twisted around. "I am, I'm sorry." She plumped down and touched his hand. "Thank you for saying I'm smart."

"Okay, then." Mark was suddenly turned on. The women viewed him as a creep, an animal. If he was an animal, he'd claim it. He wanted Sarah more than he could stand. The hotel room had been too safe, that was the problem. Mark paid the bill and hustled Sarah out of the restaurant. They hurried back to the Tide 'n Time and got into his car.

They drove on winding, hilly roads, the headlight beams fuzzed with moisture. Sarah slid down beside him, laid her head on his lap with her eyes closed, pressing the fragmented shell beads against her skin, her body given to the rising and falling. She hadn't meant to anger Mark in the restaurant, but she didn't want to be reminded of school or report cards. It was summer. Summer was for adventures, for feeding ducks. As they drove on, Sarah had no idea where they were going. It was a journey into mist, like something in a movie. When they arrived, she imagined, he'd stand and cup her face in his hands, and he'd smile with his eyes before they kissed again.

Mark stopped the car by the side of a road and they entered a path between trees that dripped with moisture. This was a private place he knew from his college days. Down and up, around he led her. The smell of pine and of honeysuckle was like a summer drink.

They came to a freshwater pond. Here the mist had not penetrated, but sharp, onyx night erased the distinction between land and water. It was too dark to see anything. Mark groped his way to a fallen log in a clearing, holding Sarah's hand. The scent of fresh water was mingled with pine. Mark dug out a cigarette to calm down.

"I thought you said you were quitting." With the flare of the orange flame, Sarah felt dismissed. "I'm sorry," she added quickly. But he had promised her at the end of the school year. Promised.

"Give me a break," Mark said. His face was stained with light when he puffed, but Sarah couldn't read his mood. She played with her bracelet, sitting hunched on the log. She raked her hand through clean pine needles, inhaling the scent that reminded her of family camping trips before her mother got cancer. A few months before she became sick, the family had been driving on the highway. It was the same weekend as the Woodstock Music Festival. Sarah's mother got a big kick out of the people in their painted vans and old station wagons. She waved out the open window, the lit Winston between her fingers a sign of solidarity. Sarah's mother used to paint watercolors. Now Sarah pretended she was finger painting with pine needles on the floor of the world; tomorrow, a field mouse would wander in the tracks left by her gigantic hand. When Mark stubbed out his cigarette, she wondered if he would take her in swimming, but she didn't want to. It wasn't safe in the dark.

The teacher fingered the Trojan in his pocket. The thought of finally coming inside her with his knees ground into the pine needles made moisture spring into his hands. Then he heard voices coming toward them from the direction of the pond.

And he smelled something. "Ah, shit," he said. "Somebody's..."

Sarah smelled it too. She thought of her brother at his friend's house, both of them getting high on grass. "Ooh," she teased, thinking that Mark was being too much the disapproving adult. "Someone's being bad."

"Quiet." Mark nudged her. "Listen."

She sat forward in night so thick it pressed on her eyes. She saw nothing, not even the man beside her on the log. Splashes came from the pond. People were entering the water in that utter dark. A high laugh skittered across the pond. It sounded like teenagers.

Maybe two of them, maybe more, and they were swimming now.

From the water, a boy's voice called out: *"Wait up. I'm not sure I can..."*

"Greg, you're such a wimp." From the direction of the girl's voice, Sarah placed her ahead of him in the pond. Her mocking tone made Sarah sit up.

The boy's wavering response came, but Sarah couldn't make it out.

"Chicken!" The girl was louder than before.

"Lisa. Wait. Lisa..." The boy named Greg choked, and there were more splashes.

Sarah's heart pounded. Two teenagers were swimming in darkness, swimming past her, although it could have been through her, because she felt that she and the teacher were invisible, lacking substance in the dark. She edged toward the water.

Shit, Mark thought. I was ready this time. Mark had not heard the boy's actual words: He knew only that swimming kids had distracted her. Mark swelled as he sensed her walking away, and the fact that these kids could potentially discover them made him crazy for her. Mark stood, reaching, wanting to sweep aside her mane and touch the fine hairs at the back of her neck. Readiness was something you had to catch before it fled and mocked you.

"Please. I can't make it." Greg's voice in the dark was fading.

*"You aren't **that** stoned."* Sarah heard limbs churning, words falling in arcs. *"Catch up, catch up,"* Lisa sang.

"I can't make it, I..." Water water.

"What are they saying?" asked the teacher, but only to find out where Sarah was in the dark. He bumped into her by accident and grabbed her waist. He slid his hands up her shorts and grabbed her flesh.

Sarah couldn't see the teacher, and she fully concentrated on the boy in the water. She yanked away from Mark and waded into the pond.

"Greg, you are so lame." Lisa's voice was out ahead, pulling through the water in the dark pond in the woods with no moon.

"Oh, my God, oh." The boy, now halfway across the pond, sounded younger than Sarah's brother. Maybe younger than me, she thought.

"Oh, I'm drowning," Lisa's voice mocked. She churned the water, and the sound was like tearing a wet sheet someone had grabbed in her fists.

"Please," the boy called.

Sarah pulled away from Mark's hands. "Greg! Keep swimming," she commanded, sending her voice out over the pond.

Laughter churned with water sounds. Greg was silent.

"Keep swimming!" Sarah felt strong. The teacher wanted Sarah so much, he could thrust it all the way up to her navel. He groped at the piney air, seeing nothing, too bad if the kid in the water wasn't a good swimmer, but there was nothing anyone could do in this dark. Kids had a way of working things out, after all. Mark was ready to come against the grain of his pants. He jammed fingers in his pocket for the Trojan, and when he was done fumbling, he groped for Sarah in the dark. Now. Now.

Sarah had no idea of the size of the pond. "You can do it," she called out. "Keep swimming." She felt power coming from her, as her naked cry went out to Greg, who was invisible to her in the water.

The other girl's mocking laughter stopped.

The darkness felt like part of the silence, as the world paused, waiting to see if Greg would make it. The boy gasped his way across the water. Slap, slap. The woods breathed.

"Keep going!" Sarah's hands were fists. She was buoyant and upright, and she wanted to run like hell as soon as she knew that Greg was safe. She had never before saved anyone.

The teacher's hand bumped her waist, and he grabbed her, but he slipped on pond muck and lost his balance. They both fell. Sarah rolled away from him, thrashing toward shore. Mark grabbed her knee when she accidentally kicked him in the face. He pushed her down by the shoulders. There was water and sand in Sarah's mouth as the teacher yanked off the button of her shorts, his knee painfully on her wrist. The bracelet had snapped, and one of the beads cut into Mark's forearm.

"Greg!" Sarah called. She kept her head out of the water as the teacher worked her shorts down to her knees. Sarah was helpless in the shallow, silty water, but she knew that her voice kept the boy afloat and moving forward. *"Keep swimming."*

Mark shoved her head down, but her face was still clear of the water. She spoke with enough rage to carry her for years: "You bastard."

Casual Day at the Crazy House

My father had been living in the bathroom for about five months, and I was in the kitchen, helping Gammy truss a chicken. Gammy has her ways. She uses the old, plain Quaker speech.

"Olivia, for heaven's sake. *Thee* knows what I mean. Hindus very *often* have those pop eyes. I find it very distracting."

"Gammy! That's so racist!"

"I'm just stating a fact, dear. You haven't seen enough Hindus."

I glared at the chicken. In those days, I didn't know how to respond—to her or most people.

The only potential Hindu I knew had just appeared, mid-semester at Cliveden Friends School, in the *Shakespeare and Madness* English elective I was taking. Katy Patel didn't talk much. Her eyes snapped with unreadable thoughts when Mr. Seaver blahed on about Lear's madness being a journey towards intimacy with Cordelia, but they definitely did not pop.

"Um," I said. "Maybe Dad will like Dr. Krishnamurthy anyway?" *Shakespeare and Madness* wasn't explaining my father to me. Shakespeare's crazies were either faking or they pretty much brought it on themselves. I thought Ophelia was kind of a twit. My father wasn't filled with hubris or sick with love. He owned a big moving company whose motto was, *We Bring You Home*, and before things went wrong, he liked to fart around in his vegetable garden.

"Damn arthritis," Gammy muttered. A chicken leg kept popping sideways.

I took the string. "Let me."

She slapped my hand. "I don't know yet about house calls."

"Ow," I said. "Ohh." Everything hinged on house calls.

"I had to be clear on whether Dr. Krishnamurthy was the *right sort of person*," Gammy explained. "Pull that tighter, please."

"Is he?" Gammy's ridged fingernail pressed and I tied a knot.

"*Was* thee listening? I half expected the man's eyes to swivel independently, like one of those lizards. I shall have to meet with him again."

"He wrote that book on people's weird obsessions. What more do you need to know? And why is everyone so *Quakerly* about this?"

"If thee means *careful and thoughtful*, I accept the compliment."

"Gammy," I bent and kissed her. "Thank you for doing this."

"Somebody had to." She opened the oven door. "Now. Thy father has requested Cheezits."

I ran upstairs with a bowl of crackers. My mouth was dry with anxiety. I almost tripped onto my parents' king-sized bed; Mom's Feng Shui again, restlessly moving things.

Dad was looking out the window, gazing at the neighbor's slate-roofed house. The trees sprouted early leaves like bright, pale parsley. There was nothing to look at. The old couple who'd lived there had gone to a retirement community, and Mom said their family was fighting over who'd get the house.

"Dad?" He didn't move. I noticed his bald spot was getting bigger.

"*Dad.* I've got a question?"

"Everything changes," he told the window. Then he turned. "Ah, Livvie." His smile looked like it hurt. I gave him the Cheezits. "My thanks. Have a seat." The chair Dad offered visitors was the toilet, but I never sat there. He slept in what used to be a large, old-fashioned bathtub before he moved his bedding in here. He kept clean in the freestanding shower, which otherwise held a rack with extra clothes. "Cheezit?"

I shook my head.

Dad sat on the bathtub's edge, munching and sad. "You'll graduate soon." He sounded like I had stage-three cancer.

"Ye-*ah*..."

"How's that English seminar going? Seaver still as sharp as when I had him?"

How would I know? "Maybe." Dad used to take me out, comparing restaurants. Then poof. Last October in the middle of roast lamb and vegetables, he stood up white-faced and gasped— as if he'd suddenly remembered something—knocking over his chair. He straightened it and left the room. Mom went right on with her story about a stray bat in the Assisted Living wing where she worked.

I'd been paying half attention to her as I listened to Dad pacing the floor above us. Gammy's eyes didn't shift from Mom's face, but her smile was too fixed; all her attention was with him.

Within a week he had moved into the bathroom. There, thanks to wireless and his cell, he continued running his company. Nobody seemed to think all this was as weird as I did. "The energy in the house is imbalanced," Mom had said, pushing out a laugh. Gammy got an inward look. "There always *was* more to him. Give it time."

Now he grinned at me like the old Dad. "So you and Zach are officially a non-item. Any other young men on your horizon?"

"No." My heart flipped like a fish.

"I'm sure they notice you."

"Dad. Are you coming to my graduation?"

"Oh, honey…" He stared into the Cheezit bowl. I pounded the doorframe with my fist, felt it crack a little, and slammed down the stairs.

Gammy was in the open garage, sweeping, so I held the dustpan with a painful hand while she manoeuvred in dust and leaves. "Look." My voice wobbled. "Forget Dr. Whatziz-name. I don't *want* Dad at my graduation."

For a moment, her eyes went soft. "Thee," she said, "is still too young to know *what* thee wants in the end." I squeezed my hand, trying not to cry. "Has it occurred to thee that others are concerned about thy father?"

"I know," I muttered. I figured Dr. Bug Eye's treatment wouldn't work anyway. And next August, I'd be gone to Cornell's hotel school. Or Boston U. Come to think of it, my safety school, in Arizona, was looking better. A thousand miles away. My father went to Cornell, and I really didn't want to have Old School talks with him in the bathroom. I emptied the dustpan as Mom's car swooped up the driveway.

"Dinner!" Slamming her door, Mom held up a container from Sushi Palace as if she'd bagged an antelope. "Hello, Mother," she cried. "You needn't cook tonight." She gave Gammy an air kiss, which Gammy swatted away like a June bug, muttering about *proper* food. "Hey!" Mom tootled her fingers at me.

Her leather boots pock-pocked on the asphalt, her coat billowing. The way my dad put it was: *Jeannie coordinates the hell out of those volunteers.*

The next day after school, I sat with my friends Sarah and Zach and this guy Phil—who they both irrationally liked—at the crowded Starbucks near Cliveden Friends. Zach and I had dated, briefly, until neither of us could stand our parents saying how *cute* it was that we'd "been together" since preschool.

Katy Patel was at a far table with some other eleventh graders. Her posture was perfectly straight. I had never realized before how seriously beautiful she was. Next to her, the other kids seemed greasy and snaggle-toothed. She hung out with different groups. I'd heard that Katy wasn't sure she liked Philadelphia; that she was thinking of living with her Dad in England.

"Rachel said Katy really had a bruise," Zach was saying. Zach's sister Rachel was Katy's friend. "Katy told him to fuck off. He was a dog, man."

Sarah touched my arm. "Liv. What's wrong?"

Katy got *hit*? "That shrink hasn't called back my grandma," I told Sarah.

"You want to leave?" she asked.

"Nah," I said.

Zach leaned forward. "Rachel said Katy hadda get stitches."

"On her ass?" Phil honked.

"No effin' way," Sarah said. Her face was horsey and skeptical.

"She *showed* Rachel," Zach insisted. "This NYU dude cast her in his movie. He was pissed because Katie came here when her mom got the Penn job. He got *real* physical." I looked over again. Her skin was kind of glossy. I couldn't imagine it bruised.

Zach spoke to Phil. "Rachel says that someone told her, Katy thinks you're hot."

"Oh, come on," I said. In the Upper School talent show, Phil had been last in a line of people who passed a chewed-up banana, mouth-to-mouth.

"I'll text her right now." Phil grabbed my cell phone out of my hand. "What's her info?"

"Cut it out!" I yelled.

"I lost my phone," he protested. "I'll text her for you." I took my cell phone and flipped back my hair. "Let her decide how hot you aren't."

Phil's grin swelled all over his face.

Zach punched her number into my phone. My hands were shaky, so I did the message in my lap. I tried to rush and had to redo it.

"While Phil's *young*," they teased. I pushed Send. We sipped our drinks, and sort of casually looked in her direction. I held my breath. Katy dug out her cell phone and stared at it. She didn't look at Phil, but her gaze, searching out mine, was smoky and troubled.

"Yikes," Zach said. "*Pwned*, Phil." Zach was a gamer.

"Not looking good," Sarah agreed.

Actually, I didn't ask Katy about Phil, or any other guy. What I'd written was: *do u know a dr krishna murthy?*

At Katy's table, the other girls were talking, heads together, but she looked down at the table. I suddenly remembered her full name, taken from the letter of introduction recently sent to school families: *Katyayani Divananda Patel.* "Let's leave," I told Sarah.

The next afternoon, I sat in the back of the classroom before *Shakespeare and Madness.* The shabby room buzzed with talk. Katy walked in, looked around, and—my chest hurt—she approached me. Being seated put me at a disadvantage, height-wise, and her serious manner made my face flame.

Katy's lips parted, hinting at white teeth. I admired her self-containment. She held her books against her chest, her feet precisely together. "Why"…she asked, "do you think I would know Dr. Krishnamurthy?" She spoke with a slight English accent. Her eyes were paisley-shaped, velvet. Mistrustful?

"I don't know," I gulped. I didn't say: *Ethnicity. What's in a name?* I felt I was suspended over something both humiliating and fatal, like an alligator that would rip my jeans off before it ate me. Losing it, I grabbed from *Romeo and Juliet.* "A Hindu by any other name?"

Katy stiffened, and her eyes, harder, took on a silver light. "Did someone tell you about Uncle Rudy?"

"He's your…?" .

One side of her mouth smiled. "Dr. Rudy Krishnamurthy? He wrote *Obsession and the Art of Balance*?"

"He's—? Does he make house calls?"

Katy gave the opposite of a sigh—a little snort. "Why d'you want to know?"

"This person in my family's got a problem," I muttered.

"Ohh," she said. "Your father? Well, good luck. Uncle's a good shrink." I should have figured Katy would know about our resident crazy man. Her curt nod made her seem older. She tripped on a backpack in the aisle, but recovered her poise with a skip, and her silky hair brushed across her nipple. In a moment of panic, I realized: I longed to touch her hair.

"Wait." My face was broiling. "Does he make house calls?"

Her almost-smile was the color of pomegranates. "I don't know." When she shrugged, one of her eyebrows quirked higher than the other. She waved at Sarah, who had just come in, and her fingers fell through light from the windows.

Katy would probably go tell her uncle to avoid us like the plague, I decided. I couldn't have made a worse impression.

"Listen up, class," Seaver called out. The buzz dwindled. "Class! Livvie here wrote in her essay that Ophelia deserved to fall off the deep end because she was a wimp who let Hamlet push her around. Was this Shakespeare's opinion as well?"

I had changed my mind about Ophelia's breakdown after I heard about Katy's old boyfriend, but a few of the girls in the class stared as though I might slither out of my seat and bite someone. *Foul deeds will rise.* Katy looked at her notebook. Sarah made a pity-mouth at me. I gouged a pencil into my desktop and wondered if the whole class could tell I was falling in love.

That afternoon, Gammy was a familiar, welcome sight. I found her clearing out winter sticks from the flowerbeds behind the kitchen. I bent and kissed her. "That shrink?" I said. "It turns out his niece goes to Cliveden Friends."

She hauled herself up on the rake. "A Quaker connection! I knew he was sensible. He returned my call today." She handed me the rake.

"Therapy won't work," I said, wanting her to argue.

"Olivia. I will not dignify that comment with a response. In fact, he is very busy. We'll be lucky to get him here before May. Now watch those hyacinth shoots."

I raked, standing where I couldn't see the sad, winter-shriveled garden my dad used to keep.

Midnight. I had jogged two miles, finished Calculus homework, plucked between my eyebrows, made notes on Baudelaire's *Hymne à la Beauté*, and I was listening to Frou Frou's *Let Go*. I tried to imagine myself as a college student, based on campus visits Dad and I had made last year, and I couldn't even remember which beige-painted cinderblock dorm room from our tours actually went with which school. Dad had made me laugh by imitating a backwards-walking college tour guide. Our family hadn't done anything regular in months. Katy's mother was in brain research at Penn, but I'd heard she took Katy to shows in New York.

Sarah's dad made huge breakfasts every other Sunday. Okay, her parents were also divorced, but that was at least normal. Zach's father had pushed him to give up game design and apply in pre-law, which sucked, but it was *normal*. I almost wished my Dad was a prick. Then I'd have a reason to be angry. Earlier this year, he helped cook for my community service project. How hard could it be for him to haul himself out to my graduation at the same damn school where like six generations of our family had graduated, him included?

Instead, people would be looking at me and Mom and Gammy at Commencement, all sympathetic, as if he was dead.

Saturday was Community service day, and I woke up two hours early. Outside, a crow clung to a scrawny, bowed-down branch, hunched there in the stupidity of everything. I knew I wouldn't get back to sleep.

Downstairs, Mom was already gone, the bed made. Out power walking, I guessed. Gammy snored through her closed door, and I looked in on Dad. How could he sleep in that freakin' tub? It was a nest of quilts and pillows. His knees mashed up against his chest. He wore the dark blue pajamas I had brought up nicely wrapped up last Christmas, after we opened our gifts downstairs. There I was, about to fall out of the incubator of Cliveden Friends, where I'd been since the age of three—*Welcome to your adult life!* He *had* to be at my graduation. What if Dr. Krishnamurthy was booked up? What if there was a fire? Would Dad let himself get flambéed?

I pulled his quilt off. His face was a smear of confusion. I grabbed under his arms. "Dad. You can do this."

"Jeannie?" He blinked.

"It's me, Dad." He didn't resist until I shoved him into the bedroom, and he grabbed the doorframe. He was more than half asleep. I pried his hands off and he fell onto the bed, his hands up as if in surrender. "Welcome to your room. Remember this?" I grabbed a photo off his bureau. "We went places?" Our family in

Maine. Another of Disney World. He sat up. He looked at the floor, not at me, and I felt relief at that.

"Mon Dieu." He was shivering. *"Je vais mourir."* I didn't know my father spoke French. Ever. He looked up, pleading and soft. Shaking. He leaned over and retched onto the floor.

"Dad. You're not going to die." I kept going because I was scared. "We're going downstairs." I took his arm.

I was pushing him when the bedroom door banged open. *"What is thee doing?"* Gammy's eyes were blue fire, and her hair stood up wildly. She wore her dead husband's plaid bathrobe.

"Mother!" My dad took a step, then he collapsed, smack on the Persian rug.

I cradled him like a fallen Lear.

Gammy's poise was eerie. "Olivia," she ordered. "Out." I retreated to a corner. She bent, stiff as a scarecrow, helping him up.

"Dad?" He looked around, vague and ashen, not seeing me. Gammy guided him into the bathroom. I got a towel, Lysol, cleaned the floor. Ran a load of Dad's laundry that Mom had left on the washing machine. I was in charge of cooking for a soup kitchen at school that morning, and I couldn't be late. I took a shower up in my solitary garret.

It was a long, stuffy day in Cliveden Friends' Meetinghouse kitchen. I had always enjoyed running the show, but Katy Patel showed up with a couple of others. I did my best to ignore her, but once I caught her eyes as she flushed, then she sort of lurched to the sink. The others goofed around, dropped pans of stew intended for the homeless, forgot to peel the carrots. I didn't have the heart to yell at anyone for leaving early. I washed all the dishes.

When I left for college, wherever that would be, I'd have to say goodbye to Dad in his bathroom. I hadn't been away from home much—not even to summer camp. If only both my parents would take me.

If only Dad would wrap his arms around me in my dorm room and say trite Dad things. But I figured that even if he forgave me, I'd scared him so much he'd never come out.

I got home at three-thirty with raw hands and a sore throat, thinking I'd picked up some dishwater virus. Moodily, I boiled water for tea.

Gammy limped in. She wiped her hands on the apron over her gym suit. "Well," she said, smiling. "I have you to thank. Dr. Krishnamurthy was terribly interested that thy father spoke in French. He'll be coming by tomorrow."

"On Sunday?" It hit me. Gammy had said *you*.

"Livvie. I hardly think the man will be attending *church*." I was forgiven, though. She felt my forehead and finished the pot, adding medicinal herbs. "Thee needs it," she said firmly.

I meant to check in on Dad, but I felt so sick after Gammy's tea that I snuck upstairs and dozed. It was rotten of me, but I wanted to apologize to a father who didn't live in the bathroom. I woke when Zach texted, inviting me to his house. Sarah was already there—no Phil—so I left a note and walked over there. We had pizza then saw a slasher flick, but I slept through a lot of it. I was looking out the window to avoid the apocalypse at the end, when I saw Katy Patel getting out of her mom's car with Zach's sister Rachel. They stayed outside after Dr. Patel drove off. Katy scratched underneath her hair, which was literally darker than the night. She was smoking. Smoking! Those pearly lungs!

"Rachel says Katy thinks you hate her." Zach stood at the window, drumming on the sill. "What's up with that?"

I sighed. I was sure Katy thought I was a complete douche. "I don't know," I said. "I'm sick. I need to go home."

The next morning, my skin felt hot and papery. "One o'clock!" Gammy announced. She had skipped Quaker Meeting today and sat at the kitchen table, chewing a chicken leg for breakfast. "But don't think thee is going to sit in and listen."

"Gammy, *please*," I said. "Is Dad okay?"

"Thee had better keep away," she fussed. "That Hindu probably lacks protein in his diet. He might get sick." I went upstairs to apologize to my Dad, but he was sleeping in his bathtub. I set my alarm for 12:45 and lay in a watery doze. What if he was really sick, with a brain tumor? Maybe he'd start speaking nothing but French, then go into a coma. If Dr. Uncle Rudy could just get him to come to my graduation…

The alarm jolted me. I tiptoed downstairs, out of the house, and down the driveway. Mom roared past me in her car, waving cheerily, back from the health food store. Surely she knew Dr. Krishnamurthy was on his way. It pissed me off that after Dad moved into the bathroom, Mom wasn't more upset. She buzzed around like a windup toy, moving furniture, trying to Feng Shui him out. My head hurt. Near the sidewalk, I lurked behind an azalea bush where Gammy couldn't see me from the house. The budding magenta flowers looked like silk. I wondered if Katy Patel knew how to wrap up in a sari. Her hair was as shiny as the black car that bore down the street toward me now, going slowly, as the driver checked for house numbers. An icy reflection of sky slid across its hood. I was afraid Dr. Krishnamurthy might miss the house. I sort of popped up from the bush, remembering I'd forgotten to brush my hair.

He pulled up by our lamppost. Still hiding, I motioned him toward me. He was very short, and he walked expectantly. His clothes were crisp business casual.

I introduced myself. He shook my hand matter-of-factly, as if I were Dad's receptionist.

He did have prominent eyes. I hated myself for noticing. "Um, could I ask you a question?"

"Yes, sure." He put his hand to his chin.

"I'm thinking my dad might have a tumor or something. Like those people you read about who think other people are hats and gloves."

"Hmm. I'll need to see him to ascertain if he thinks I'm an umbrella stand."

"Right." I hesitated. "I know your niece from school."

"Ahh," His face lit up. "And your name is…?"

"Olivia."

"Yes. She wasn't happy at her old school."

If I didn't have a fever of a hundred and three, I wouldn't have blurted out: "You think she'd want to hang out with me?"

Dr. Krishnamurthy gazed at me with a practiced neutrality that shrinks reserve for the truly demented. I hadn't showered, my face was oily, and a pain behind my left eye was making it twitch. "I don't see why not. Now," he added, "Please take me to your father?"

"I can't," I said. "I'm hiding from my grandmother."

"Ah…" he said. I felt like one of his patients.

Dr. Rudy's visits became a regular thing. I heard from Zach who had heard from Rachel who had heard from Katy that he wasn't charging us very much. I told myself that the fact that my father was in therapy improved our normalcy rating. Everyone's parents had been, or were, or *would be*, seeing shrinks. Never mind that ours sometimes stayed for three hours. Or that laughter erupted from the bathroom. They'd hit it off, and Dad seemed less anxious. Once, my mother told me, she caught him rummaging in his bureau. "I almost screamed," she said, laughing to death, "at the sight of a man in my bedroom." There had been no more speaking in French. I didn't let myself get too happy, though. Until Dad was able to leave the house for medical tests, Dr. Krishnamurthy emphasized, we couldn't rule out brain involvement.

During that time, I worked hard at my classes. I wanted to show my dad straight A's. Once, Katie grinned at me over Seaver's recitation of *Tom O'Bedlam*. Talking to her was something else. She wouldn't make eye contact, and I couldn't help thinking that she knew her uncle had been holed up in the bathroom with my weirdo father.

One Sunday, I was in the kitchen re-reading my acceptance letter from Cornell for the thirty-seventh time, when Dr. Rudy came down, rubbing his hands together. "Now," he said. "Where do you hide the tea?" He no longer wore jackets, but usually button-down shirts. Today, a polo. Casual Day. I got the Darjeeling and filled the kettle.

"How's Katy?" He was smiling.

"Huh?" I said.

"She hasn't made any particular friends yet." He picked up the canister. I wondered about Rachel. Come to think of it, they weren't together at school a lot. "Proper tea. I like that." Sweet odors floated in from the back yard, where Gammy's roses climbed the garage wall. I looked Dr. Krishnamurthy right in the face, my heart thumped once, and I spoke her name out loud: "Katyayani Divananda Patel." It vaulted through me like a bird taking flight.

"Very nice accent," Dr. Rudy said. I'd had no clue about an accent. He pumped my hand. "Your father told me about Cornell. Congratulations!"

"It's just the hotel school. Here's some shortbread." I arranged wedges on a little plate, fast. "Dr. Rudy. My graduation is in three weeks."

"I know."

"You do?" I'd been afraid to broach the subject with my dad, simply glad that he had forgiven me. Grateful, anxiously hoping in the shrink's abilities, I carried his meals to the bathroom and took in Dad's Cornell nostalgia. Once, he said, "You know, Liv. The ass-kissing Greek life isn't for you. You're better than that."

"Of course you want him there." Dr. Rudy's hand on my shoulder was so tender that tears stung my eyes. "We'll have to see how it goes."

Half an hour later, I heard them laughing. If Dad was crazy, crazy didn't sound so bad. Some nights,

Mom slept on the bathroom floor, showing support, and, I knew from the muffled sounds, more than that.

I stared at my phone. I swallowed and made myself write a text. *U want 2 hang out this Fri?* I lay on my bed and felt like vomiting. After a while, my phone buzzed.

yes sure was Katy's answer. *it sounds like fun*

A few minutes later, she texted again: *Sorry I was weird I thought you didn't like me I keep wanting to be just regular*

I didn't know what she meant. It didn't matter. I got up and ran all the way down the stairs to the first floor. Then I ran back up again. Gammy was coming down. I kissed her, then propped her against the wall.

"Thee had better have a *good reason* for this," she scolded. I ran to the kitchen. Mom sat there, paging through a book on therapeutic crystals.

I grabbed the book. "You don't need this!"

"Hey!" she called. I ran upstairs again. Dad came out into the hall, bemused and flushed. I kissed his forehead and started up to my room.

On the fourth stair, I stopped dead. Dad looked up at me, with a small embarrassed smile. I didn't know what to say. He lifted two fingers, saluted me, and turned around. By the time I got to his bathroom, he had closed the door. Dr. Rudy congratulated my father like he'd just come down from Everest.

Their voices were warm and familiar. "It's a matter of acceptance," Dr. Rudy said.

"Stability is there," my father replied. "But if you try cling to it..." I slid down slowly with the door against my back. I could feel them talking. It was silly to get so excited over a new friend. Maybe Katie and I wouldn't hit it off. Did I dare let her know what I really felt? I was leaving for college soon. My father might still have a brain tumor. No one had promised he'd be there for graduation.

As for me, I was regular: not *Katyayani*.

I whispered the beautiful name. Something like a flower bud opened in my chest.

Pertaining to My Arrest for Indecent Exposure

My father died three weeks ago, but the burial was delayed because of frozen ground.

The night of his death, my sister Emily called at four in the morning. "Chip? He's gone." She could barely speak through her grief.

I waited till she calmed down. "Thank you for telling me," I murmured, not wanting to wake my wife.

Emily let out a shuddering breath, then quietly hung up the phone.

I lie in the dark most nights with my wife Linda asleep beside me, thinking about my father. My body is tense. I feel like a cheap rug that will always have wrinkles and never lie right. Although I have to face a room full of tenth graders in the morning, I don't begrudge the lost sleep. It keeps him alive in some fashion.

Soon after I was born by emergency Caesarian, the story goes, I stopped breathing. A rare and wise woman doctor rescued me and made me briefly famous, as I was the first newborn in history to be kept alive with a respirator. My father bullied his way into the room where I struggled. He stayed there without sleeping for almost three days, afraid to touch me, until I recovered.

After Emily was born without incident three years later, screaming bloody murder, my father hired an infant nurse. This was even though my mother's Tennessee mother and grandmother were on the scene and armed with nasal aspirators, blankets, Vaseline, a bathing tub, strong calf muscles, and an auto-rocking cradle with a crank that sounded like a ratchet screwdriver. My dad was convinced their flowery perfume would give the baby asthma. Though he had not been wounded in World War II, he had known lots of men who were. He trusted a woman in uniform.

My clearest early memory is of the great snow of 1966. It doesn't often snow here, but school was cancelled along with classes at my father's university. Mom and Emily were swaddled on the couch while Mom read a cozy story about children in rural Canada in winter. The book described a wonderful treat, and we wanted to try it. I shoved on my boots and ran outside to scoop snow into bowls. In the living room, we poured maple syrup into the white mounds, which melted the top crystals. Maple snow tasted wonderful, as if the pristine winter forests of Canada had been boiled down to their essence. The thought that such delight could fall from the sky entranced me.

Our father came downstairs at that moment. He stared, puzzled, then his face reddened. "You're letting them eat snow?" He grabbed my bowl, then Emily's. She shrieked. He dropped one, ignoring the slush on his feet. "What about the nuclear testing? They're ingesting fallout!"

"I didn't—how would I"...our mother tried to explain.

Dad dumped the remaining snow outside. Emily was gearing up for one of her famous tantrums, so I ran upstairs with the treat reverting to ice in my stomach. Confused, I dove under my covers. After Emily quieted down, I heard my father rant, "Do Chip's teachers think that cowering under a desk will keep the kids' flesh from burning off?"

Mom said something soft and urgent. Emily whimpered.

He snorted. "'Duck and Cover.' What a joke! This is a brave new world we're in." I left the bed and crawled beneath it. I liked the 'Duck and Cover' drills at school. They made me feel safe. Dad went on, "I'm not trying to scare them. These weapons are our protection. But you can't treat them like child's play."

That same night I dreamed that vivid orange snowflakes were falling outside. Emily danced around, wanting to make snowballs, but the flakes burned holes in her jacket. She laughed in amazement as steamy pits hissed on her puffy sleeve. When I yelled at her to come in, she looked around. That was when the snow hit her face.

I kept the dream to myself, but for months I pestered my dad to build a bomb shelter. He wouldn't hear of it. "The Soviets might be our enemies," he said, "but they aren't stupid. Just don't eat snow."

Perhaps in reaction to Dad, our mother is a hugger. Even her sentences are hugs. When I was a kid, I used to work on model airplanes in the kitchen and listen to her talk on the phone. Many people called her with their troubles, but to me it seemed as though she had one generic phone-call friend, who was a conglomeration of random adults. Now I realize she spoke in platitudes. Still, people seemed to find them as comforting as I did when I overheard her. After all, they kept calling. "It never rains but it pours," she'd sympathize. "But things always work out for the best, God has His plan." Sometimes I heard, "I know your mom/granddad/cousin is in a better place" (this often with a swift glance in my direction). She would purr, "Bye now," with the same soft exhalation with which she still energizes her enveloping, pillowy hugs.

When my father lay dying in hospice, she lost interest in everything. The house got messy, and when she wasn't visiting him, she lay down on the sofa. She only had energy for hugs. She managed to give the impression of full body contact while keeping air between her and Dad. "He doesn't have enough stuffing for me to squeeze it out of him," she mourned.

Dad was buried in a driving sleet. Beneath a dark green canopy, my teenage girls shivered in their ankle boots while Linda and I held hands. Emily and my mother stood with their shoulders touching. Emily's four-year-old son Damian was with his father for the weekend. My dad's colleagues and former students huddled toward the grave, trying to keep the drip-line from hitting their necks. Father Martin read from the prayer book.

Emily had brought two dozen scarlet roses and she began handing them out. I recalled how close we had come to burying her that time she was in high school. I held my flower while people stepped forward for a last look at the coffin. The flowers made streaks of red as people dropped them in. My mind felt frozen, but I was uncomfortably hot; a trickle of sweat formed at the small of my back. My daughters threw their flowers, and then retreated from the maw of the grave as if the ground would tilt them into it. My mother dropped in four or five, kissing each one softly. You couldn't hear the roses land on the casket over the hissing sleet, but they lay on the coffin like smoldering coals.

Except for the family, the mourners had departed. Father Martin, a small, chilled man, bid a hasty but not inappropriate farewell, shaking everyone by the hand.

My mother turned to me, trembling with cold and emotion. I gripped the woody stem in my gloveless hand. It would have been better if the thorns had not been cut off, leaving harmless nubs. I was stiff, almost paralyzed, yet I found myself hugging her.

"This is your final farewell," my mother chided, stepping back and giving my flower a nudge.

Like hell it is, I thought. Even Linda's questioning gaze did not send me forward. My daughters stared.

Emily stepped between us. "It's okay, Mom," she said. "I understand." My mother laid her head on Emily's shoulder, and I stared at my sister. *I* didn't know why I'd held on to the rose. How could *she* know?

The girls fell into confused giggles.

While my father was in the early stages of treatment, I used to go sit with him in the evening. He perused academic journals while I leafed through the magazines on the coffee table. After I had asked how it was going and he replied *As well as can be expected*, we sat in silence. I skimmed my magazine and thought about how he had stayed beside my incubator when I was a newborn struggling to breathe.

I agreed to meet Emily at Starbucks a day or two after the service. "Are you okay?" She already sipped black coffee.

"I think so," I responded. "How are you?"

"So-so. Damian's been crying for days," she said. "He got his whole class to make condolence cards for Mom."

"That's sweet." I felt a little embarrassed, thinking of my two girls sitting stoically grim during the service and burial. Linda had made them send cards; otherwise they wouldn't have. I wondered if Emily knew this. They *are* teenagers, I mentally argued. Their grandfather's death messed with their perception that if your hair is long and straight enough, you can kick death in the teeth. "What did you mean when you said you understood about that rose?"

Emily didn't exactly answer me—or maybe she did. "I'm worried about you," she said. "It's important to grieve."

"For Pete's sake. How *should* I grieve?" I'd hardly slept, thinking about Dad. Was there some emotional algebra that escaped me?

"It's not a *should*." Emily winced at the scalding heat of her black coffee, but kept sipping it. "I mean it's a very individual thing. But it's not healthy to refuse to feel. You know how Mom and Dad are. Were. *Are*. Oh, hell."

"I *feel*," I protested. "We just buried him. Give me time." Our father had carefully crafted his dignified stance. It would have felt wrong to react to his death in a way he found unseemly. Mentally, I checked my insides. I wasn't exactly sad. I felt…What *did* I feel? The previous night I'd been troubled, thinking of the roses streaking like comets into the grave. I woke that morning and felt mostly relief. It was over.

"I know it takes time," Emily said. She bent over as if her stomach hurt. "On the way here, I accidentally drove into the hospice parking lot. I was really sad I couldn't go and see him, and then I felt terrible, because if he was still there, he'd be suffering."

She looked thin and pale. I recalled that moment when we were teenagers. Emily had clung to me like a small child. I'd pulled a sweatshirt over her and rocked her in my lap. When my girls were babies, I couldn't hold them without thinking of Emily in her nakedness.

Emily's come a long way since then, and I'm proud of her sobriety and her job managing a bookstore. Yet the family spiraled downhill after that dinner a year ago when she dropped her bombshell. We were at my parents' house. Dad carved the roast in his expert, practiced way, and no one knew that his substantial brain was already initiating a chain reaction of cancer cells. After the apple crisp, my sister pushed aside her untouched plate. Her eyes were spangled with tears and nervousness. "I have something to say." Emily got up and closed the glass doors into the hall. "I've been writing a book. An agent accepted it, and she says there's a good chance it'll get published."

"Congratulations!" Linda cried. Engaged in action figure carnage out in the hall, Damian made explosive noises with his mouth.

"What kind of book?" I asked.

"It's about me." Emily smeared mascara with her white linen napkin, and shot a sideways glance at our father. I could see my mother trying not to notice the napkin.

"A *memoir*?" Linda spoke with a thrill.

"Kind of."

Our father cleared his throat. "What category of literature is it exactly?"

Emily looked him in the face. I saw that her arm trembled. "It's the story of how I got sober. It's about how I was raised to squash emotion. It's about being the child of a war-traumatized soldier."

My father turned white.

"Oh, dear God." My mother burst out. "That *wretch* Hitler. The Japanese. It's all their fault." She touched my sister's wrist, and Emily clutched her hand for a moment, then let go.

Linda leaned across the table toward my sister, as if ready to catch her tears.

Our father had taught his college students about Aristotelian catharsis, but this was different. Emily was exposing *him*. Calmly, he said, "My dear. Some things are too intimate and difficult to be expressed without linguistic safeguards."

"Oh, now," Linda protested in Emily's defense. Linda's parents had met at Woodstock. She hadn't fully realized when she married me, an older man, that Emily aside, she was inheriting an old-fashioned family with old-fashioned ways of not saying what we really meant.

"What is that supposed to mean?" Emily challenged him. "You think I just randomly decided to spill my guts? You think I didn't *think* about this?"

"It isn't just *your* guts," I intercepted. I felt as if I had been punched in the stomach. Imagine how my father felt.

An unusual amount of chaos ensued. I don't remember much of Emily's argument—except that she accused my father of failing to trust her instincts as writer—and her ensuing departure, plastic muscle men flying and protesting three-year-old in tow, but after it was all over, my father and I sat alone at the table like frozen men.

"Will you try and talk her out of it?" I asked.

He was very composed, but perhaps for the first time, he looked truly old. His eyelids were pouchy. "That would only provoke resentment. It's her book, not mine. She's an adult. And a good writer." He added, "She'll have to live with it."

I wondered if he would cut her off. What I asked was, "Are you all right?"

"I made a *choice* not to talk about the war." That was his only answer.

We did not discuss the memoir again as a family. My parents were cordial and a little distant with Emily. We no longer had family dinners. We exchanged Christmas presents as before, and once Emily told me she was grateful that, despite her book, our parents still sent her occasional support. I didn't ask if she still planned to publish the memoir. By that time, Dad was sick, and I had other things to worry about.

Actually, Dad did mention World War II once. Emily was in ninth grade. Avoiding the preppy clothes of the day, she affected hippie dress, which didn't endear her to the status-conscious student body at our high school. She started accumulating rock 'n roll and protest buttons on her military-style shoulder bag, and these attracted our father's attention one evening when she came home from a friend's house.

He grabbed her bag, which she had dumped on a kitchen chair. "'Ban the bomb?' Where did you get these?" The bag might have contained a dead animal. "'Kill the Nukes?'"

She twisted it out of his hands. "Sto-*op*. It's just a joke."

"A joke?" His laugh was bitter.

"It's ancient *his*tory."

I was about to tell Emily to can it, but my father shocked me. He grabbed her shoulders and pressed her into a chair. She was so surprised that she didn't fight him. "My dear, you don't know what you're talking about. I was slated to be sent to the Pacific. The casualties would have been astronomic. The only thing that saved my bacon was when your so-called 'nukes' were dropped on Japan. You wouldn't be here without them."

Emily gaped. She slipped from his grasp, laughing. "I wouldn't be here! I wouldn't exist! Yay! I wouldn't exist!" She danced around, her bag whirling behind her. She must have been high. My father walked across the kitchen, took hold of her arm—he was a big man—and slapped her across the face. Emily stumbled, then ran out of the kitchen, shrieking. She stayed in her room all weekend.

I don't know if further words were exchanged between them. I don't know if our dad ever apologized for slapping her. Emily became quiet and secretive, coming home as little as possible.

I was in graduate school the first time Emily went to rehab. She did three stints before she stopped using drugs. She met André, Damien's father, on her second pass-through.

After Emily almost hanged herself in eleventh grade, our father stayed home for three weeks, like a silent watchman, until she returned to school. It happened on a Saturday while I was home from college for spring break. I thought no one was home. After leaving to meet some friends, I found I'd left my wallet behind. I drove back and ran upstairs. In the hall, I stopped. A sound made me think of a dog pulling against a leash. "It's Emily," I realized. I don't know how I knew. Emily was then scornful of everything around her, but I wouldn't have called her depressed. I don't remember flying up the stairs, but my mouth tasted weirdly of metal. The cedar closet door was open. The shock of her was a bright flash. She had driven in a nail, used an old clothesline, knocked over a chair. Her hands groped upward, like a blind person trying to catch a fly. Her hair was over her face.

I leapt on the chair, hoisting Emily up. I ripped the knot from the nail. We slid to the floor and I gathered her in my lap. She was limp, curled toward me. "I love you," I repeated, rubbing her back. "Come on, come on." When she started to shake, I was so relieved I cried.

Only later did it hit me that my sister was fully naked, and that her body was very beautiful.

Apparently, she had left a note for our mother. Mom told me later that Emily's unorthodox dress and casual behavior at school had given her a sexual reputation that far outstripped the true, virginal facts. *You want me naked? I'll give you naked.*

Our parents treated me like a hero, which offended me. Emily was aloof with me for a long time—how do you talk to your brother about something like that—? But a year later, she wrote me a letter, thanking me for saving her life.

I didn't save Emily's life. It was a fluke that I happened to return home that day. Perhaps the knot would have broken under Emily's weight (it was worn). Perhaps she would have saved herself—she reached for the rope as I found her—and my role meant nothing beyond the fact that while lives can be lost by accident, so, once in a while, they might be reclaimed by accident.

Until Emily informed us about the memoir just before Dad got sick, we thought all she wrote was poetry. After she became pregnant, she split up with André, dropped out of college, and gave birth to my nephew, a birth without crises. I am aware of the irony of that statement. But it was a healthy—and according to my mother—a joyful birth, a new beginning.

When Damian was a baby, Emily found a job in an independent bookstore. My parents helped her out financially, although I never knew to what extent. "It's the least we can do," our father put it when he explained it to me. "I know you'll understand, Chip." I valued his estimation of my character, and I can honestly say I never resented their support of Emily.

Just after Dad was diagnosed, she told me she'd dedicated the memoir to him. The hardness in her face reminded me of his. "You can't do that," I protested. "He got sick just after you told him about it."

"Don't accuse me," Emily said. "Telling the truth does not cause cancer."

"Are you calling your family liars?"

She came right back at me. "Are you saying I made him sick?"

"Emily, I know Dad. He'll read it out of duty. It'll only cause pain." I couldn't accept that he wouldn't live to see the book. I was furious with her, but I wouldn't stoop to say so.

"He's the one who needs it the most," she insisted. "Remember what he told us about Hiroshima?"

"Do *you* remember?" I challenged. "You were high as a kite."

"He said that without the bomb, he would have been sent to die in the Pacific. It scared me," Emily admitted.

"You danced around the room when you heard it!"

"That's because I was so scared."

I protested, "No one knows if the bomb saved his life."

"*He* believed it, though," Emily cut in. "He said our existence depended on it. Imagine what it was like for him, living with that. One family against a whole city getting vaporized."

"But he was dignified about the war," I protested. "He didn't wallow in it."

"Since when is there anything dignified about war?" she demanded.

I was silent. Our father was sick. The last thing he needed was to hear that his children weren't speaking to one another. When I spoke, my voice shook. "You'll do what you want," I said. "But I will never read your book."

I knew I wouldn't need to read it. I had already seen my sister naked.

Now Dad is gone and I lie awake, thinking of the red slash of flowers against the dark coffin. I'm stifling hot and I can't stand the covers, while Linda hunkers down under her side of the quilt. I didn't visit often after Dad went to hospice. He was stripped of more than his once-robust white hair: his humanity. He looked withered, twitching slightly, yellow-skinned beneath a faded blanket. By not watching with my family and the hospice people, I spared him the observations that the healthy cannot help making in fascinated proximity to death. I gave him something far less than they did, but something nonetheless. Emily was upset with me, but I didn't defend myself. I think he understood. I spared his dignity. Linda went more often than I, and we had been married long enough that she didn't push me.

One Saturday, no one else was in his room. I turned over his knob of a hand and laid my head on it, kneeling by the bed. "I love you," I said once while he slept. The words felt strange but right.

Emily had brought an extravagant bunch of pink flowers. They loomed like a huge ghost baby on a nearby table. I thought they were lost on him, but it was a nice gesture. Gently, I tried to wake him. "I'm here, Dad."

His eyes became unstuck, sought me out. He muttered something. His mouth was so dry I couldn't make it out. "What? Do you want some ice?" I was hoping he could still talk.

He turned his head and looked toward something in the room. "That cloud."

He was seeing things. I didn't know how to respond.

"Pink," he said. Then, very clearly, "A rotting stench."

"Is there anything I can do?"

"Take it away."

Helpless, I looked around the room. The hospice was a renovated Victorian house. The room might have been in a sparsely decorated B & B. I stared at him, stricken.

The only new thing around us was the bouquet of flowers, which I picked up. "Is this it?" I detected a nod. "Dad, Emily brought these."

"No. No." His agitation made him grimace, and he looked inhuman. "The explosion." The doctors had warned us about hallucinations. I put the flowers out in the hall and stroked his forehead until he lay back and closed his eyes.

After a while, I took the vase down to the nurse's station.

It can happen that way with brain tumors, I explained to Emily. She'd arrived to visit Dad just as I was walking to my car. Remember what they told us? It's nerve damage.

"Oh, my God. I thought he'd like them."

"You couldn't know," I said. "He's not himself."

Emily hesitated. "Maybe he's more himself now."

"What do you mean?"

"He said the flowers 'exploded'? It sounds like it might be some kind of memory."

"Of *what*?"

She considered. "I'm not sure. Something about the war."

"Do you have to psychologize everything?"

"No," Emily told me, "I don't. But he might feel guilty that we survived because of Hiroshima."

"We weren't there!" I protested.

"We grew up under its shadow."

This struck me as a criticism of the kind of father he'd been, yet there he was, dying. I was so offended that I walked away and drove off, without another word.

I saw my father twice more. Instead of flowers, Emily brought a beautiful Asian wall hanging. She donated it to the hospice after he died. My father was unresponsive at that point, but I hope he noticed it.

Shortly after my father's burial, I drove home from school feeling ill, as if my skull was packed with insulation. I poked myself in the face, but instead of feeling anything, I heard a deafening crash. I sat gripping the wheel, wondering why the windshield was a road map of crazed glass and broken wood. My wife and daughters rushed outside.

I got out and assured them I was fine. "It's next door," I said. "Their propane tank must have blown up."

"You drove through the garage door!" Linda cried. "Are you all right?"

"I feel quite well," I responded, surveying the wreckage. Come to think of it, the neighbors didn't have a propane tank.

"Wow, Dad," my daughter said. "Are you a whack job?"

I had to take control and reestablish normalcy. I phoned the insurance company, then insisted that we settle down to dinner as usual. Linda's lasagna had no taste, but the oddity of a flavorless dinner gave me something to concentrate on. When the phone rang in the kitchen, Linda, who wasn't eating, jumped up to answer it. She came back looking tight-lipped.

"What is it?" I asked.

She hesitated. "It was Emily." My sister hadn't wanted to trouble us while Dad was dying, but it turned out that her so-called literary agent had made her cough up three thousand dollars for "necessary edits" and then disappeared.

"That's good," I smiled. "No more book."

"Da-*ad*," my oldest protested.

"That's so mean," said the youngest.

Linda regarded me in a way that is impossible to describe.

I needed to get some air. I stood up. "I'll be back in a few hours."

"What?" Linda startled. "Where are you going?"

I felt as surprised as anyone by my declaration, but it was important to offer a rational explanation for the fact that I had to leave. I spoke the first words that came to mind. "I'm going to offer Emily moral support."

My wife and oldest child spoke at once. "You shouldn't *drive*," Linda said.

"I'll take you in Mom's car," my daughter said.

I shook my head. "A stroll will do me good," I said, pulling off my tie. The house felt stifling.

Despite Linda's pleas, half an hour later, I arrived at Emily's. We sat on her sofa. "That agent is a criminal," I said. Damien slept in the next room, and I kept my voice low.

Emily smiled, but the skin under her eyes looked bruised. "You've already said that three times. Are you okay?

"I'm worried about you," I insisted. "People take advantage of you."

Emily fingered her necklace. "I'm fine. I'll publish the book. I have to."

"I wish you hadn't written it," I said.

"I know you do." Her face was open and frank.

"Do you really want to expose yourself for everyone to read?"

"I'm not exposing myself. I grew up feeling exposed and unsafe. I tried to kill myself because I wanted Mom and Dad to recognize that."

"Mom said you did it because kids were mean to you at school."

"They *were* mean to me, but that's not what I told her."

"She said you left a long note about school."

Emily's snort reminded me of Dad's. "My note was addressed to both of them. It had only one line. A question: *Why am I so different from you and Chip?*"

"Well, I suppose Mom found what happened pretty hard to deal with, so she"—

"You don't have to defend her." Emily gave a short laugh. "The irony is that if you trace it far enough back, you were the one who gave me permission to write this book."

"Excuse me?"

"That time in the closet. After I tried to kill myself and you were holding me? I actually felt glad."

I stood up. "Oh, Em"—

She grabbed my sleeve. "You didn't know what I was going through, but you *saw* how much it hurt. And you held me. Until you found me, I just wanted to rub Mom and Dad's face in my anger. But when you were so tender, I was able to feel the actual pain. It was a big relief. It was the truth, and it healed me."

Heat prickled behind my eyes. "You were naked," I observed.

"Dad talked about Japanese children with their flesh burned off. I thought dying with my clothes off would be just as shocking."

"Dad was naked as he died," I observed. "Is it hot in here?"

Emily touched my face. "Sweetie, you're crying."

"Everything that made him Dad was gone." I saw him withered and white, like an embryo of death.

"I better call Linda," Emily told me. "I'd drive you home, but I can't leave Damian."

"I'd rather stay with you," I said. "Tell me about your book."

Emily smiled. "Another time. I promise."

Something inside me was cracking open. I was hot; I was having an earthquake.

"You know what?" I asked my sister. "I think I'll walk home. It'll do me good."

"I don't think—

"Now don't worry about me," I interrupted, putting on my coat. I blew my nose. "You just figure out how to get that book published."

"Wow." Emily beamed. "Thank you."

We hugged. She was solid and warm.

For a moment, I stood in Emily's open door. My back felt the heat from her house, and light spilled on the concrete steps, which sparkled with falling sleet. I closed the door and called Linda to say that Emily had offered to let me crash on her sofa. "I'm fine," I said. "I feel much calmer." An evergreen bush grew beside the steps, and I twisted off a branch. Since I missed giving Dad the rose, I thought, it's time to lay a tribute on his grave.

I wanted to feel the sleet on my skin. I took off my coat and left it on the sidewalk in front of a nearby house. Walking fast in the freezing rain.

Sleet falling over the cemetery, on my father, on me, from a dull orange sky. Ice and wind mingle with warm gusts from these lit-up stores. Inside I'm hot, molten, while my skin's in shock from the cold. I discover I'm crying. I have to tell him: I need his boxed formality and Emily's passion and my mother's enveloping hugs.

I unbutton my shirt and fling it aside, then, stumbling, I ditch my pants. It's not enough. I throw my underwear and shoes in the street. I walk, and I embrace his silent courage and Emily's stubborn spirit, and if it breaks me in pieces, I will be in pieces.

A green light sees me through the intersection, not far from the cemetery.

Holding the yew branch toward the sky, I run toward my father.

ABOUT THE AUTHOR
Helen W. Mallon

Helen W. Mallon grew up in a Philadelphia Quaker family. She attended Quaker school and has an MFA in Writing from Vermont College of Fine Arts.
She reviews books for the Philadelphia Inquirer, the San Francisco Chronicle, and other venues.
Helen is a writing coach and leads creative writing workshops in the Northwest Philadelphia area.
http://helenwmallon.com

Author photo: Julia Staples

47166023R00067

Made in the USA
Middletown, DE
18 August 2017